Warning! Socialism is Poison to Liberty

Warning! Socialism is Poison to Liberty

Charles E. Miller

To order additional copies of this book, contact:
Xlibris Corporation
1-888-795-4274
www.Xlibris.com
Orders@Xlibris.com
84211

SOCIALISM IS POISON TO LIBERTY

LETTERS TO A CITIZEN

ONE

HOW THE SOCIALISTS WILL DESTROY THE BILL OF RIGHTS

Citizen:

From THE DECLARATION OF INDEPENDENCE: "We hold these truths to be self-evident, that all Men are created equal, that they are endowed by their Creator with certain inalienable Rights, that among these are Life, Liberty, and the Pursuit of Happiness—that to secure these Rights, Governments are instituted among Men, deriving their just Powers from the Consent of the Governed, that whenever any Form of Government becomes destructive of these Ends, it is the Right of the People to alter or to abolish it, and to institute new Government, laying its Foundation on such Principles and organizing its Powers in such Form as to them shall seem most likely to affect their Safety and Happiness . . . ." That second paragraph is of utmost importance in the interpretation of the US Constitution.

First: Rights are an endowment by our Creator, not an enactment by the State
Second: they are inalienable; therefore they cannot be taken away by the State.
Third: the phrase "among these": indicates that there are more than "Life, Liberty and the Pursuit of Happiness."
Fourth: Those additional rights are contained in the first Ten Amendments to the Constitution, adopted and passed and signed at the same time as the first VII articles of the Constitution. They are known as The Bill of

Rights. They are intended to protect the people from the possible dangers of a tyrannical government. Any tyranny, present or future, will attempt to remove those inalienable, God-given rights that block attempts by tyrants to gain power over the people, like a king.

Fifth: Government derives its "just powers" from the "consent of the governed," that means from the consent of the people, not from fiats or regulatory laws or vendettas or political policies of the governing powers directed against the will of the people.

Our founders were pragmatists. The Bill of Rights is a pragmatic document that protects the people from oppressive government. An oppressive government ignores the will of the people as the source of its power and direction . . . Any government constituted of self-willed demagogues is an oppressive government and, by the authority of this document and the instruments of voting and voting obligation the people are authorized to change that government to one that supports their will and the ends of their freedom, life, liberty and the pursuit of happiness.

"Among these" means that there are other inalienable rights other than "Life, Liberty, and the Pursuit of Happiness."

"Certain" means they are specific as described in the Bill of Rights

Those inalienable rights, the "among these" rights and the "certain" rights, are set forth in the Bill of Rights. Don't take the Founding Fathers for fools.. Their Bill of Rights bore a specific and enumerated connection to their Declaration of Independence. They are given by God to suffering mankind. They cannot be altered or removed by the Congress or by the Supreme Court, or for that; matter, by any Lower Court or individual citizen.. When and if that proactive "firewall:" is breeched, the State then resorts to anarchy, the self-will of demagogues who lust for power, and the attribution to the people of irrelevance at law and dependants in entitlements. This shift of the basis of power from the people to the government is tyrannical. In a free society, it comes about by slow accretions of power to the demagogue tyrants and unnoticed loss of power by the people. This transference of power depends on the silence of the media—the voice of opposition.

AMENDMENT 1—"Congress shall make no law respecting an establishment of religion, or prohibiting the free exercise thereof; or abridging the freedom of speech, or of the press; or the right of the people peaceably to assemble, and to petition the Government for a redress of their grievances."

A right is to be distinguished from a privilege. A RIGHT is an endowed by God, not by the State . . . as "endowed by our Creator with certain inalienable rights of life, liberty and the pursuit of happiness." Subjection of the people by a tyrant is not conducive to happiness, and certainly not to the preservation of life and liberty.

INALIENABLE means they cannot be taken away from the people by any political, religious or social entity!

A PRIVILEGE is a concession by the State of a liberty to practice a certain more, code of honor, customized way of life or controlling regulation. That privilege is created and tolerated by the State. It can therefore be withdrawn by the State. Grounds of "neutrality" are the inevitable reason for denial of the assertive practice and observance of that right. There is no language in the First Amendment that commands neutrality, but only freedom (of conscience) to observe that endowed right. Absolute neutrality can be attributed only to the dead. The contemporary imposition of the doctrine of "political correctness" to insure neutrality is illusory. It insure only mediocrity by placing artificial constraints upon free speech, giving no quarter to expressions of religious faith in the public forum, and mocking superior performance as blasphemous to the (religious) Statte, as talk radio, Limbaugh, Hannity, Beck, Coulter, Levin, et all. Those constraints ultimately lead to "thought police" in the name of "equality."

A right and a privilege are in no way identical in origin or in mutability, changeableness. God is the origin of the first; the State creates and enforces the second by regulation. We have especially in a socialist State the Divine ordinance v State regulation and control . . . God is the source of secular rights as endowed rights, such as freedom to peaceably assemble and to petition redress of grievances.

Tyrants of the State will deliberately confuse the two sources of power in the minds of the people. In that way, as controllers of the State which is ever jealous of its (their) power, the politicians and liberal judges will attempt under socialism to seize a right which they cannot do because of this Amendment. The total eradication of prayer in schools becomes an abridgement of a right, not a privilege, as the Supreme Court in Engel v Vitale) has done. Prayer in schools is the free exercise of a religious faith by the individual student citizen. It is not an attempt to establish what already exists . . . 'the free exercise thereof." The socialist state is pleased with riots, which tend to destroy the endowed right to peaceably assemble. Thus the liberal court grants to rioters the privilege to sue the police as imposters on their liberties!

A right to display the Ten Commandments in a public forum is an originalist concept, not an invention by the State of a privilege which can be withdrawn, as it has been done already by the Kentucky Supreme Court (in. Stone vs. Graham) upheld by the liberal US Supreme Court.

A right to pray at graduations is a freedom of religion, not a State concession of a privilege or a toleration of a privilege. Toleration of such expressions means that the State and not God controls the "establishment of religion" and "the free exercise thereof." The right to express one's faith in a public forum is a God-given, endowed right, not a State concession of a privilege. The court therefore, erred a third time (in. Tanford v Brand) the State's operative word is "neutrality" in these expressions of faith in the public forum. Were the Founders mindless of this public expression, or did they conceal a darker secretive purpose to confine prayer and displays of biblical truth to hidden venues of church and the underground? Account then for the numerous religious statements on public buildings in Washington DC. Neutrality?

The mention by Navy Chaplains of Jesus Christ, stricken from communion and from biblical lessons and from ceremony, is an abridgment of religion; The Supreme Court has extinguished that right as a privilege denied Satanism is now given credence as a religion in the military services. The further secularization of our society will bring State censorship of talk radio, cyberspace, university curricula, and private conversations. The people of a formerly free society will then be at war with their socialist government.

Since the State, represented by these Supreme Court rulings, have adulterated the meaning of Article One, the State has presupposed itself the equal of God and in fact, performs the function of God as the source of the Amendment, not the God of Judeo Christian religions. The socialist State replaces God as the provider of essential human wants and needs of the 21st century. God is generous; the State will ration. God inspires creativity; the divisive State punishes creativity as a threat to its power. God gives men free will animated by moral conscience; the socialist State is suspicious of free will as an impediment and danger to its power.

The Supreme Court, representing the State but is independent of the Congress, has skirted, indeed, has broken the law of the First Amendment by which Amendment I the Congress is given negative authority of preclusion and abstention. An authority NOT to perform a certain act—the prohibition thereof—contains the same moral value as the authority to do an act, take a position, make a statement, and protect a right. The thesis of a prohibition implies the antithesis of an endowment in the context of Amendment I.

What have the socialists to do with the above argument? Socialism posits a State that is ever covetous, ever jealous, ever preemptive of power to control the people. That control includes the religious practices. Presently the Supreme Court has confused a right with a privilege in this matter, the practice and the demonstration of religion,. The Court has acted in the above rulings and similar rulings, that it can usurp the right of endowment from God and prohibit, under penalty of fine and or arrest, enforce its personal, as distinguished from jurisprudential will, upon the people, in violation of Amendment One. Liberals and Leftists have used the Courts to legislate in their behalf, preempting the power of Congress to so legislate, as set forth in Article One.

Therefore: Prayer in school, at ceremonies, displays of the Ten Commandments, moments of silence in the classroom, is permitted under Amendment I. They are not attempts to set up, to establish a religion, which is what the First Amendment means. How can these entities substitute for the Congress? The First Amendment was not written for atheists, satanists, agnostics, or non-believers of any sort. They are all Americans, however, and are entitled to the protection of the laws. To expunge a First Amendment right protects no one. "Neutrality" imposes the religion of Secular Humanism on the classroom. Man in the form of the State becomes the god for students. Man's agnostic will supersede the Founders' design with the intention to expunge God's endowed Right.

Now that prayer has been outlawed—in its specific meaning of appeal to God instead of to the State—we go to the elimination of freedom of speech. The Socialist State intends to remove all potent, viable objections to its policies, and thereafter if not sooner, make ready the State to accept a tyrant in the office of the President. Freedom of speech, including of the press, is the first Right to go in any dictatorial regime. Silence the opposition is the rule of the State's iron-fisted demagogues, and then enact laws that will totally eliminate free speech and its genesis of freedom of conscience in the name of totalitarian unity. The innocuous symbol for that tyrannical unity is "political correctness." The route is through legislation from the bench. The direction is to create detestation of Christian conservatives. And the end result is the surveillance mechanisms of a totalitarian State in which the people no longer have the protection of the US Constitution because of Statist outlawry. Surveillance?—by Obama's Czars, for starters. Then children snitches, paid informants and gullible follower disciples of the regime . . . all in once-free America.

A false or fictitious freedom of speech is achieved by force, the State through its radical courts compelling the eradication of certain anti-Statist comments, statements of political positions, in order to accept the equality of the Statist argument in the name of fairness. For example, equality means the striking down of superiority and the uplifting of inferiority. . The people in a Socialist state delude themselves that they still acknowledge superiority by their devotion to sports and sports figures. That mindset, if you will, was why Nero proposed games in the coliseum for the entertainment of the people . . . so that would forget their barbaric/entertainment subjection. The fairness doctrine will impose this draconian obligation on those voices which now offend the State. The State should never be offended? Come now. This intrusion of socialist leftist views in an effort to diminish and to destroy conservative, right-wing political views is not competition in the name of unity. It is compulsion in the name of State triumph over the consciences and the character of an entire people.

Freedom of speech is always, always the first right to fall before the juggernaut of statist Socialism because its conservative opponents promise, pretend, threaten republican-democratic opposition to the power of the State.

Opposition to the socialist agenda—Socialism of the Marxist sort is absolute control of an entire nation, not just the means of production—depends on freedom of speech, unabridged by the jealous State. Freedom of the press is included with speech, since the press generally represents print speech applied to this elimination of free and open speech. The liberal press, silent in the decline of Amendment One liberties, reinforces illiteracy and the silence of the great numbers of illiterates in America estimated to be some 20 percent. The silence of mainstream media shows both indifferent to and ignorance of the disappearance of this fundamental freedom and Right because like the illiterates, they refuse to speak out about the obliteration of free speech in America's classrooms and in the public forum, generally.

The right peaceably to assemble is controlled not by the State, but by the right of the people to express their grievances. Peaceably. That is a critical word . . ."peaceably." Not with rocks, bottles, fists thrown at the police by punks in the name of justice, which the liberal court recognized as a rightful but not a peaceable assembly, the police in the view of the court, being the instigator of the rocks and bottles in the park. The court even allowed the rioters to sue the police, who were there to keep order. not o incite to riot.

In doing so, the Lower Court demonstrated its incompetence as a judicial body and its willingness to work as an adjunct riot group to aid the rioters against law enforcement. Each incident like that erodes the guarantee of the right of free speech, the press, and peaceable assembly. These laws, which liberal courts have consistently ignored, preserve a civil, peaceful society for the rest of us. The attitude is to break the law if justice is rendered by their personal opinions. That is the road to anarchy in America. The one tool or instrument of peaceful conciliation that remains to the people is . . . to impeach the justice. Although some the liberals among them may think that they are God's anointed, they are hells conscripts. When I was a kid, we read newspapers in the classroom to acquaint us with the operation of free speech in actuality.

The bottom line of the First Amendment is: that Rights are endowed by our Creator and are inalienable. They cannot be removed by a court of law or by the Congress. Privileges are State generated and can be given or taken away by the State. The two—RIGHTS and PRIVILEGES must not be confused. They are not identical. The application of the neutrality grid to adjudge the cause of action is a false test of freedom in practice and in the courts. .Neutrality, like conscience, is relative in today's system of legislative court justice. It means the total exclusion of a right to express one's faith openly, not underground and out-of-sight, as if subversive of a free society. Socialism will further undermine the First Amendment. We will soon have a Supreme Court Justice who believes that under certain circumstances a book can and should be banned! She will reflect the President's view on the matter of book-banning.

NEUTRALITY is an illusion created by liberals who rule through legislating courts to enforce NEUTRALITY. Absence of a Right in practice is not neutrality but, instead, is the absence of access to that Right, which denial is not neutrality but is the prohibition by legalized prejudice .intended to reflect the control of the State. Violent riots do not deserve the protection of the First Amendment, which requires that the assembly be "peaceable." Rocks and bottle missiles are not either "free speech." or "freedom of expression." The petition of a grievance is civilized and constitutional. Missiles are an appeal to anger rather than to the reason of a "petition of grievances" .to the "government." A socialist state will support the rioters by appeasement of the rioters and their sympathizers. Power to control by an ideology the law-abiding citizenry is the objective of a Socialist state. The Ideologues of that State accomplish their end by intimidation, which takes the forms of fines, increased taxes, rationing, and entitlements. There is involved a heavy element of bribery, political pressures exerted in secret deal-making beyond closed doors.

Be wise. Resist and pray for God's providential help!

TWO

SOCIALIST STATE TO SEIZE GUNS IN VIOLATION OF SECOND AMENDMENT

Citizen.

The socialist State, anxious to make itself God, protector and source of all virtue before the people, will attempt to destroy the second Amendment because the possession of guns by the people represents a threat to its omniscient power over the people.

AMENDMENT 2: "A well regulated Militia, being necessary to the security of a free State, the right of the people to keep and bear Arms, shall not be infringed."

This is a right endowed upon the people by their Creator God, one of the "certain" specific rights included in the phrase "among which" found in the Declaration of Independence. The purpose of safety is fundamental to a free society, the protection of the people. The Founders had had enough with British armies and did not in this Second Amendment; ordain that a standing army should be formed up.

Rather, it was their thought that owners of guns being responsible citizens could be deputized to defend the State, since there is no place in the Constitution in which a standing army is explicitly established. After the revolution, when the Constitution was written, many of the people and some of the delegates were already well-trained. A "militia" infers the people's readiness to defend their country. A militia can be well-regulated i.e. trained if its members possess firearms. Remember that in WW II, we trained with broomsticks at military bases.

God is a warrior and is jealous God to protect what he has provided for those good stewards with faith in Him. A "free State" is a State without an oppressive government or a tyrant King. A dictator. The word "free" is significant. It means in this context free of tyranny in any form and free insofar as its citizens enjoy their endowment of freedoms enumerated in this Bill of Rights.

Therefore, when we look at the words of Amendment 2, we find that the word "keep" is significant. KEEP means not to stow the arm, the gun, in a distant armory, not to loan it without conditions, not to give or to barter the firearm away or to hand over to a government bureaucrat. "Keep" means just what the word means, to hold onto, to secret, to place in one's possession logically in the home.

"Bear arms" gives the liberals and leftist socialists trouble. They presume that the bearing of arms occurs when the well regulated militia is formed up. That is partly true, but they kept arms then make their appearance in the form of a deputization for their use by a state under assault or anxious to preserve is integrity, its unity and soundness and its continuation.. The colonial leaders The militia referred to is an invisible militia of gun-owners. The Founders were anxious that the people be able to defend themselves . . . perpetually.

Therefore, the arms indicated in this Amendment are for defense of a free state in order to keep it free—the purpose.

Traditionally, Americans are hunters, Americans are Protectors (2nd amendment) and Americans are enforcers (militia to enforce border laws). But . . . Americans traditionally are not avengers.

It is upon that pretext and thesis that the State attempts to deprive the citizens of his weapon, that he is an avenger and will not use his weapon to defend his freedom. That is the responsibility of the State. The people are too irresponsible to possess a firearm. Socialists deem them too stupid to know how to use a gun properly, or even to understand the second amendment as a Right.

The State will attempt to confuse protection with a vengeance and thereby, morally justify, being all-virtuous, criminalize the right of the private citizen to keep his gun in his possession. The kind of a weapon is a ploy to defuse the anger and resentment of this draconian abuse of State power.

The substance of this Amendment therefore is that the private citizen is endowed (again) with the right to possess a firearm to protect his freedom which, multiplied by the total citizenry, means the State, not the individual, is the sole possessor of the freedom of gun ownership. . Read the Amendment. The Founders planned that the individual use his gun to defend himself and his family and his property so that they remain free.

The gun is abused to murder as an act of revenge, vengeance and avengement. The State uses that perversion of the amendment right to justify its collection of guns, its regulation of ammunition, its requirement of gun design. All of these are to give the power of gun ownership and protective violence to the state, not to the citizen, in violation of the 2nd Amendment. For where any prohibition is placed upon gun ownership to the advantage of the State, he State seeks not the welfare of a free citizenry but the power of usurpers, the thieves of a God-endowed right that belongs to the citizens. Resist.

The citizen, endowed with the right to keep a gun and to bear it to preserve his freedom, has an inalienable Right to keep his arm for his safety, his freedom and his very life. Possession of an arm is the specific "certain" right, another of the "among which" referred to in the Declaration of Independence. It is a Right that is or can be a means to his continued "Life, Liberty and Happiness." The socialist State preempts that right by concocting regulations that essentially and in time will expunge that right. Resist.

How the tyrannical socialist state will enforce that order, to collect all guns, leads to the State's destruction of the next Amendment 3. Installation of an electronic device rather than habitation of a soldier can be the requirement for all homeowners in the future. Big Brother wants to know what you are up to! That action is known as a "fishing expedition" into our personal lives. Spendthrift Governor Schwarzenegger has begun the shift by requiring that all California homeowners install a CO_2 monitoring device in their homes. We must get used to having the State invade our lives more than they already do. A CO2 monitor by State law placed in the home? Then will come entry by law to read the monitor. Then will come a mandatory camera to further enchain the individual to big government. The resilience and patience of the people is exceptional, because we are an exceptionalist nation. We, the people, may appear to the arrogant politicians to be soft and pliant and stupid when, actually, we are just waiting for showdown time. Resist.

The bottom line is that the socialist State, ever greedy for more power to increase its size and control, will diminish the power of the people to defend themselves. Their excuse for demanding that the citizens surrender their guns is the lack of a PERMIT to own a gun. Every gun owner without a permit will be deemed to be a criminal. Every gun owner will have to have a permit to keep what they are ENDOWED to KEEP AND BEAR under the Constitution's Second Amendment. This specific endowment is authorized by the Lord God almighty, not by the State. The leftists will snivel a mock at this statement of faith and demean gun owners as "violent crazies. Since God no longer exists according to Neitche and the US Supreme Court, and .the State presumes in its arrogance to have triumphed in the matter of possession of a firearm the conservative enemy will have been suppressed and denigrated into silence. Resist.

The State lusts to be the sole possessor of the power to defend, the power to control, the power to shoot, the power to protect the people, helpless charges who are ignorant triflers with the law. The deception is that the law is no longer the law in a Socialist State. The law becomes judicial fiat and bureaucratic regulations ad infinite. The aim of the Socialist State is \ not justice but fairness, not diversity but equality not freedom but political correctness, not investment but taxation and not risk but dependency. Here is no middle ground in the Socialist State. The present southern border situation is a good example of the rigid incompetence of the Socialist State, The socialist government will control the gun owners by PERMIT. Bureaucrats will control the non-permitees as CRIMINALS. We gain strength by association. The Socialist State fears the power contained in that freedom of association, the "PEACEABLY TO ASSEMBLE" which is an ENDOWED RIGHT. Remember that the leftist courts will uphold the rioters because they are "victims" who, however belittles and that destroy that First Amendment right. A peaceful assembly of gun-owners—read "militia"—is fearsome thing to the leftists—exactly what the Founders intended. IN ORDER TO REMOVE THAT THREAT, THE STATE WILL CRIMINALIZE OWNERS OF GUNS. To enforce that law, the State will require a program of house inspections without court warrant to specify the object of the search, as provided for in Amendment IV. "The right of the people to be secure in their persons, houses, papers, and effects, against unreasonable searches and seizures shall not be violated, and no Warrants shall issue, but upon probable cause, supported by Oath or affirmation, and particularly describing the place to be searched, and the persons or things to be seized." Show me the signed Warrant, the statement of a probable cause (the why) and the exact description of my gun to be seized . . . or get the hell off my property, Redcoat!

THREE

SOCIALISTS WILL PERVERT AMENDMENT TO CONTROL CITIZENS

Citizen:

AMENDMENT 3: "No Soldier shall, in time of peace, be quartered in any house, without the consent of the Owner, nor in time of war, but in a manner to be prescribed by law."

Simple. Before the American Revolution and as a contributing cause thereof, the Recoats had ordered colonials to share their homes with British troops, the later sometimes pushing out the owners and his family entirely in order to convert the house into a barracks. At times rape occurred/ Eminent, also, was the ongoing seizure of all household goods, including foodstuffs for the benefit of the invading enemy. Remember that the Colonials so abused with the blessings of the King George III were still British citizens. This commandeering of a man's home—and essentially his life and the lives of his family—was one of the most colossal of offenses against the colonies that invaded and corrupted life altogether.

Socialists today have, presently, no troops to insult humanity and to invade the privacy of the individual. But, under Obamacare, the citizen will be forced to admit the Central Government into their homes in other ways. Let me list them:

1) Thou shalt place in thy home a monitor of CO_2 levels, to be accompanied by periodic checks by the Regime of an owner's gadget, on the assumption of cheating by certain owners thereof, as on taxes.

2) Access to private bank accounts, portfolios to determine the honesty of the citizen in reporting medical needs his insurance and his ability to pay a part of the costs. This access will be via the cooperation of banks and investment corporations, electronically.

3) Periodic checks by a Czar to determine the marital status, additional children, divorce . . . all matters pertaining to the institution of marriage will now be accessible to the Regime in Washington. Family size, as in China, will be limited by the Socialist State.

3) In certain homes, where an alleged crime is being or has been committed, surveillance cameras for certain rooms, like ankle monitors, will be mandatory (the bedroom excluded) thus to monitor a citizen's alleged defection from or abuse of an Obmacare program. The State's distrust of the citizen will be profound.

4) The utter lack of privacy, except when on the toilet, (As in England today, cameras everywhere, no aspect of life omitted) It is said that in Soviet Russia the surveillance became so severe that, in fact, persons who may have been suspect got together, colluded, in their bathrooms where freedom of association and speech could not be monitored by a bureaucrat Czar. Obama's basic purpose for the State—surveillance of the American citizenry.

'5) The requirement that when a citizen stanched his groceries in the home he will have to file a receipt as to the purchase costs if Federal money, and itemizing the kind of goods the Central Government wants to exclude, including fatty foods from the diets of all Americans.

6) A monitor both within and outside the home will track uses of energy, the ordinary billing being insufficient for the Central Government. This will be the carbon tax. The monitor can be a part of the CO_2 level gadget Solar panels will become mandatory. Use of rooms for church and home industry will be micromanaged by big government.

7) The sophistication of the above "gadget" will also indicate the use of any fuel other than butane and natural gas. No wood fires, no charcoal barbeques (in time) no trash burning . . . Evidence of these infractions will bring a fine, then a stiff penalty. Fireplaces will become merely decorative. Washington will be watching.

8) The paranoic relations of big government to the private citizen will be further increased when the Regime orders homeowners to shut off unneeded rooms because of excessive need for heating . . . as now water rationing.

9) A czar or czars will come to the home of the citizen to see that all the above modifications have been made and that the citizen is adequately supplied with brochures, documents, chats and warnings—and taxes to force compliance.

10) .But they have other means of ingress into the lives of homeowners, such as taxes that drive the owner into bankruptcy, controls on schooling, especially home schooling, surveillance cameras will record

11) The citizen will be forced to ask the ongoing question, not what will it cost me, but what will any violation cost the government and then trembles lest he be caught, fined and or imprisoned.

12) Occupation of the home by the Recoat government is not complete. A liberal court will no longer issue either injunctions against or permits for wire taps but a Czar, looking out for the governments and appointed by the dictator, without restrictions of power, will casually and at random sample phone conversations to see what is going on in the private sector. That is the upscale version of the old-fashioned party-line of the 1930's

13) As if these insults were not enough, to the utter abolition of the protection third Amendment of the Constitution, the socialist State will assign Czars to track, like gumshoes, like private sleuths, certain selected citizens to see how they spend their federal entitlement money. As recipients receive more and more food-stamp money, which are, as today, used for pleasure purposes, alcohol, drugs and gambling. There will occur less and less control on the specific entitlement because of the volume of complaints, the people now having been weaned from their former independents to a

total dependence upon the federal Government. And this is only the third Amendment

This revolution in Regime control will occur by the expedient of perverting the meaning of the last phrase of the Amendment . . ."In time of war" and "in a manner to be prescribed by law." We are at war with Jihadist Muslims and al Qaeda. (That condition is satisfied) Also, the above invasions of citizen privacy will come gift-wrapped in new laws that will further destroy the protection of the third amendment and embolden and enlarge the power of the impersonal Federal Socialist State in Washington DC. We shall see how far the Socialist State will go to enforce the "right to privacy." The one under a democratic; republic, the other under a Socialist State.

Resist. Pray for wisdom and help from a providential God.

FOUR

SOCIALISTS INTEND IN TIME TO SUBVERT AMENDMENT IV

Citizen:

Keeping in mind that the Declaration of Independence is essentially a religious-secular document—the Founders always considered that their new country would be a people of faith and not a godless people—certain "INALIENABLE" rights have been bequeathed, "ENDOWED" by their "Creator" upon the citizens simultaneously, "amongst these"—meaning there are others—are "Life, liberty and the pursuit of happiness." The others are included in the Bill of Rights, passed at the same time as the Constitution.

AMENDMENT 4: "The right of the people to be secure in their persons, houses, papers, and effects against unreasonable searches and seizures, shall not be violated, and no Warrants shall issue, but upon probable cause, supported by Oath or affirmation, and particularly describing the place to searched, and the persons or things o be seized."

The people posses this extraordinary power of possession and protection by law, regardless of what the Socialists may assert, namely that we are not a Judeo-Christian nation in origin, therefore the source of the Fourth Amendment Right, God being dead, is invalid and consequently that Right is automatically expunged and/or depending on the court is amenable to re-interpretation, that is to the law is represented by judge's personal opinion. This crucial negation of established law accounts for the romantic, intolerable phrase "a living Constitution." It is alive in the prejudiced mind of a Socialist judge. It is dead in its originalist meaning and application to the case. .The people no longer have that protection, of Rights itemized in the amendment. The Socialists have stripped away those protections by their denial and nullification of the source as God Almighty. Humanistic law is Godless; it is man-idolatrous.

'Anxious to increase State power, the Socialists denigrate and destroy the Bill of Rights Amendments one by one, piece by piece, (incremental Socialism) by these means:

1) Security is not obtained by the mere possession of a house, a sacred repository, in which the citizen lives. Sometime it is called his "castle." Under Socialism, a wooden construction is not by its very existence fit to be deemed a proper and secure repository of cherished, invaluable, personal papers and keepsakes' Nor under Socialism is such a structure deemed to be a man's castle, a fort for the security of himself and his family, a bulwark against invaders. However, this particular socialist ideology I call the "Castle Complex," a psycho-somatic condition that is delusional and afflicts all Socialists. This is especially true when the State, by its own promptings and attestations, needs to examine documents and papers that may allegedly undermine conflict with or otherwise tend to destroy its power of administration and, yea, its very existence. Therefore, as a plain act of self-preservation, the State reserves to itself the absolute invented right to investigate any subversive documents, any instruments of destruction, any terrorist or subversive schemes to destroy the tyrants of Government. This false right removes the protective power of a man's mere house. The drawbridge is let down by human desire and phony layering. Effects—prized possessions, personal letters, silverware and momentous—otherwise share the same Socialist deconstruction of alleged protection. That is a ludicrous repository i.e. castle to depend upon. The "probable cause" need not be honest. The oath can be fraudulent and the itemizing can be totally contrived in the absence of actual entry and evidence gathered. That is called a "deconstruction" of the meaning of the Amendment, and is applicable to all the Amendments.

2) Most important is the matter of the persons who dwell within the castle under siege. Ever watchful after their own security and power, the Socialists reserve the right to take a person into custody from his own

dwelling place . . . Their reasoning is simple enough: There are citizens with grievances against the State who pose a danger to the continued security of the State and, where evidence will allow, deserve to be taken into custody i.e. seized in order to prevent and forestall damage and injury to the State officials. This is especially true in matters of finance, investment, so-called free-market which are loathsome to the Socialists. Therefore, the interdiction and neutralizing of the harmful effects of this Amendment—if enforced—is absolutely essential for the State's continued governance and, indeed, for its survival. Either lay seize to the castle and seize its inhabitants, or suffer the loss of the mailed fist of the state. The charge can readily be trumped up. In fact, Sharia law permits this wide and irresponsible latitude of assault on the inhabitants of the castle.

3) Under Socialism, the assumed protection of a Warrant is a fiction long ago dismissed by the police as a rubber-stamp order for the seizing of threatening\drugs, guns or terrorist training materials kept in the castle. (This will not apply to mosques as Jilhadist training sites.) There can be no political, economic or spiritual secrets kept from knowledge of the officials of the State, appointed to be its protectors. I am not here speaking of the FOIA power as applied to legitimate State document. In the minds of State Socialists in Washington, the Search Warrant is not nor can it be called reasonable or necessary when it jeopardizes the safety and security of the State, and of course, of the people as well, an afterthought. Yet the Court Warrant with its oath and condition of description is an absolute protection for the home-owner if he happens to possess dangerous documents and effects, like guns and explosives to bring harm to officials. However, Socialists want to limit the meaning of "probable cause" to any instrument that can sabotage the State. Socialist judges will see his phrase "probable cause" as timely, legitimate and meaningful speculation! The oath or affirmation then becomes, in this context, simply a salutary expression of interest in the dangerous documents, effects and/or persons.

Why my warning? The present regime has no reason to invade my house with the intent to seize me or any member of my family, or any paper\I might possess. But liberal civil or Federal courts will not need or use a search warrant. Two or three violations of the Fourth Amendment by home break-ins by the police in search of whatever will gradually accustom the people to the use of the Castle tactic.

THE SOCIALIST STATE IS BASICALLY A POLICE STATE that paradoxically accepts man's innate goodness. Why, then, is there a need for .the police? To cleanse the state of its enemies . . . profit-takers, Wall-Street, zealots, political objectors . . .

Do not be naive about this. However, please don't misunderstand. We need the police; although Socialists are convinced that human nature is basically good—improvable by virtuous State efforts (in an institution of correction)—and therefore police disciplines are considered to be irrelevant and unnecessary. If they break up riots, they can be used by the rioters. That is the source of Socialist distrust of cops in general and hate for Christians to whom man's nature is basically sinful and evil.

Before our Revolution, it was customary for a London Magistrate to issue an order to the British occupiers of Boston to knock on the door of a Colonial house, flash their authority of the King and Parliament to intimidate the owner, and walk into a citizen's house for the purpose of searching for an allegedly subversive document or a hidden arm. Paine's "Common Sense and "The Crisis" would have been objects for seizure as subversive of the Crown. There were times that the British soldiers would muscle their way into a home without any excuse whatsoever! For food, muskets, silverware pawnable in London and rape. If this crime had not occurred many, many times, to the dismay and rage of the colonials, who were still British citizens, the Founding Fathers would not have written this protection into the Bill of Rights. Note: that security in the home is an endowment by our Creator God. It is an absolute protection. Absolute—inalienable—means it cannot be broken or annulled or abridged.

If you do not believe in God then the home-security becomes problematic for you unless, as you will, you assume, that the Central Government is the origin of that right Yet, consider, that if laws can be made they can also be broken, annulled or changed. They are, consequently not absolute, not always protective. This includes the Bill of Rights—the First 10 Amendments.. I am not compelled to be "nice." in this matter. Our greatness issues from our freedom, not from our Socialist submission to and punishment by a Central Government. No government in the world has a document anywhere comparable to our Bill of Rights . . . anywhere!

Our present Socialist regime will find an excuse, a pretense of protection...namely a search for registered or unreserved (suspected) combat weapons possessed by the householder, a subversive document initiated by a terrorist trainee, a drug operation, an illegal alien for deportation by ICE, a wanted criminal released or freed on probationary conditions . . . any excuse to violate the protection of the Fourth Amendment. A Constitutional Right is not a removable or changeable right. It is permanent to the citizen, cannot be abrogated or removed from his retention and exercise, and it demands that the government respect his claims thereto. A warrant from the proper court is required for all police actions against a homeowner with the intent to enter his domicile. That warrant represents state permission, not chief of police decision. And it must exhibit reasons and objects for the entry. No more, no less. I would defend a gunrunner against police bursting into his home without a warrant. That sets a precedent and is unconstitutional. A retroactive warrant would suffice. Without that Warrant, we participate in a police state action, regardless of how well-founded the suspicion by the police of illegal activities going on within that home. Only an emergency, like a cop taken hostage, make lawful an instantaneous and immediate entry by the police . . . or a fire in the home. An emergency. If there is not time for a warrant, it can be gotten post-action but it must exist somewhere on the record to legitimize the police action. The home is not to be the sanctuary for lawlessness. The Fourth Amendment was intended to protect the innocent and by the use of a procedure establish the lawful precedent for the future. Violation of this protection is an act of outlawry regardless of the perpetrator. Is not attempted robbery of a house a crime?

We did not think that in the Kelo case, almost 125 houses were purchase and their owners and families ousted to make way for a private developer's plans. That happened. In such cases, it is the intention of the government to increase its power and REVENUE, initiate propaganda of fear in the citizenry, and reinforce its authority over the citizens, further diminishing our liberties. REVENUE by the way, cannot be defined as "for public use" as can a road, a bridge, a municipal building. The Kelo revenue was private profits. The Court unlawfully approved of the transfer of ownership from private entities—125 homeowners—to another private entity—the real estate developer. Concentration of power without redress. The State lacked any kind of adjudicatory oversight.

Washington made it clear in his farewell address that liberty depends upon the right and equitable distribution of power as established in the three branches of government. When the court begins to legislate, we are headed for the destruction of liberty. When the President begins to exert non-Presidential powers, we are headed for the destruction of liberty. When bureaucrats assume powers not granted to them even by implication in the Constitution I (Czars. department heads), we are headed for the destruction of liberty. When ambitious men despoil the rights of the people by bad laws, dishonest legislation and tampering with juries in the interest of a party ideology, we are headed for the destruction of liberty in America. When a free press perverts and subverts factual truth as ideological opinion either by the President or the Supreme Court, we are headed for the destruction of liberty in America. The present administrative ideologues—Marxist-Socialists—adhere to the concept that the government is the source of freedom, happiness and justice rather than its tolerating by minimally intrusive laws the exercise of liberty by a free people.

The present administration is convinced that the government is the enforcer and promoter and protector of freedom rather than the claims by the people of their fundamental rights. The present socialist democrats are in the process of nullifying our and the happiness that issues from laws that apply to them as well as to the people. Our present Socialist government, like all Socialist governments, is in the process of self-destruction. Electronics have created a sense of false omnipotence. People like that are scary. When our 13 to 20 trillion dollar national debt outreaches our productive capacity, our GNP, we will have no government to speak of. A shell of the past. What them?—anarchy and revolution and violence. Our present one-party administration is a curse to this nation's freedom and her greatness. It lacks the character to endure, to struggle, to risk, to envision and to liberate. It simply lacks character, from Obama inclusive of all the members of his cabinet and the radical Democrats in the Congress. They are a bunch of fraudulent, ill-intentioned Scalawags who are destroying America's exceptionalism, her power, her beacon light before the world, her readiness to respond to the world's tragedies. Resist. Pray for wisdom and help from a providential God.

FIVE

SOCIALISTS TAMPER WITH AMENDMENT V BY VOIDING DUE PROCESS

Citizen.

This Amendment V, like Amendment VI protects the individual citizen from the State. . "No person shall be held . . ." and "In all criminal prosecutions . . . (VI)

AMENDMENT 5: "No person shall be held to answer for a capital, or otherwise infamous crime, unless on a presentment of indictment of a Grand Jury, except in cases arising in the land or naval forces, or in the militia, when in actual service in time of War or public danger, nor shall any person be subject for the same offense to be twice put in jeopardy of life or limb, nor shall be compelled in any criminal case to be a witness against himself, nor be deprived of life, liberty, of property without due process of law, nor shall private property be taken for public use without just compensation." Amendment 14 provides the same due process protection.

Socialists would strike down the phrase "due process of law." The identical protection appears also in the 14th Amendment: " . . . nor shall any State deprive any person of life, liberty, or property without due process of law, nor deny to any person within its jurisdiction the equal protection of the laws.". The reason for their voiding the phrase is not because of the process so much as that it has requirements. That is, State obligations. Socialism is an ideology that avoids obligations by the State, replaced by demands by the State. The obligations are—jury selection, discovery of evidence, legitimacy of the evidence, defense counsel, and availability of witnesses and presumption of innocence before the trial.

These requirements, or obligations, are lacking to European justice and to Sharia law. The Colonists had endured the corrupt injustice of British hegemony over justice and the Parliamentary-King aristocratic justice for almost two hundred years. The Crown's so-called justice was conducted in secret (from the Colonists) by the House of Lords and their manufactured charges long before the Revolution. Today's Socialists in Washington would use our court system to promote their ideology of State control of the accused, the evidence if real and matters of fines, imprisonment, and jeopardy. NOTE BUREAUCRATS, NOT JUDGES, ESTABLISH THE PARAMETERS OF FINES, IMPRISONMENT AND EXECTION OF THE SENTENCE, BY THE EXPEDIENT OF A HARNESSED MEDIA. THE BENCH BECOMES THE ECHO VOICE TO JUSTICE ADMINISTERED, WRONGLY BY THE UNELECTED ADMINISTRATION AND AN ELECTED TYRANT . . .

The specific protections were the issue of colonial experience with the Crown's rule and methods of administering justice to its own citizens. American courts under a Socialist regime will try the citizen on grounds that the accused has misrepresented Socialist ideology—making the trial one of political "misjudgment," instead of a rival for a civil misdemeanor or criminal felony. Thereby, the Socialist ideologues on the Bench will strip the individual of his rights of conscience in matters of oath-taking and testimony. In this manner, the corrupt ideologues on the Bench, mouthpiece of the President and posing as followers of the law, will embolden and enlarge the power of the State over the citizenry by the tactic of intimidation. The Socialist court will thus demonstrate that the accused was not deserving of the "due process" of protection because he or she was not a believing Socialist. Thus, Statism is a religion to the Socialist, as currently it is to Barack Obama, even though he is President, in name only.

The Liberal US Supreme Court will continue to express in their decisions the borrowed European presumption of guilt before innocence is proved. USE OF EUROPEAN LAW INVITES THE USE OF 9th CENTURY SHARIA

LAW. THIS ADULTERAION OF AMERICAN JURISPRUDENCE OBLITERATES OVER TWO HUNDED YEARS OF CASE AND STATUTORY LAW. UNDER SOCIALISM, JUDGES, OBSESSED BY THE CREED OF FAIRNESS, WILL BORROW FROM INFERIOR EUROPEAN COURTS. THEIR RULINGS ARE SUSPECT; THEY MAKE BAD LAW. SHARIA LAW WOULD IMPOSE THE JUSTICE OF FIXED RETALIATION INSTEAD OF EVIDENTIARY PROOF AND COMPASSIONATE PUNISHMENT . . .

The selection of a Grand Jury has much to do with the fundamental honesty and/or application of the charges of capital and/or infamous crime. Today, the public display via TV of infamous trials affect to reduce the realistic possibility of two trials for the same offense. The people will complain. A legal flaw in the first trial does not remove this public criticism . . .

Deprivation of liberty and property is consistent with the malfunction of the clauses of this final specific protection. Due process, unique to American trial procedure presumes the innocence of the accused until guilt is proved . . . upon presentation of evidence by material facts and first-hand witnesses. No hearsay. It is in the bribery of witnesses where the crime occurs, a procedure handed down by example from a Corrupt Congress, the bribery of a candidate to step aside allowing the briber to "clear the field" for the benefit of a favorite candidate. Bribery is a silent cowardly procedure initiated by the State with taxpayer money to protect its vested interests. That is why earmarks are despicable.

UNDER SOCIALISM, BRIBERY BECOMES A METHOD OF OPERATION. IT IS FOR SOCIALISTS A LEGITIMATE PURCHASE OF A SERVICE OR A COMMODITY. THE CONTEXT IS IRRELEVANT.

The accused can "take the fifth" amendment protection and therefore not stand as a witness against himself. This is a special consideration in trials that involved torture, criminal association, personal beliefs and connections, honest dealings, false charges, conspiracy, and prejudicial witnesses against the accused, not to mention "stacking the deck" of evidence and clever manipulation of language to entrap the testimony of the accused be manipulation of the evidence.

The way is open for corruption of our judicial system with Socialists in control of the government and therefore of the Court system. Under Socialism, it becomes okay to manufacture evidence to insure equality of outcome in the Court's decision. Socialist legislation from the bench enquires—a religious credo—manipulation of the law to attain a certain outcome . . . with the appearance of law. The Supreme Court and the liberal lower Courts, to insure this equality, are compelled to borrow from foreign laws in order to make certain that the judgment has a global legalistic source and status. SOCIALISM FOSTERS DISHONESTY IN GOVERNMENT BECAUSE ITS OBJECTIVE IS FAIRNESS AGAINST AN UNFAIR SYSTEM, A WAR OF IDEOLOGIES. Ever wonder why feelings animate liberal judicial decisions? 'Fairness" cannot be defined as a law but instead as a personal reaction based on feelings! Watch out!

Due process by American standards controlled by law is absent in European Socialist countries, strike the rules as to discovery of evidence, the gathering of same, the qualifications of witnesses to the case, the testimony of legitimacy of witnesses. Strike out hearsay, the dependability and trustworthiness of witness-stand oaths, oath perjury . . . and the power of subpoena. Under Socialism the State exhibits none of these safeguards to a just trial. Fairness is not determined by any of the above but by the suffering of the plaintiff at the hands of the accused. Thus the injured party becomes the perpetrator while the latter turns victim. This inversion of roles is due to Socialism's contempt for the rich, the higher in station, the capitalist parasite. SOCIALISM SCORNS THE COMPETITION OF LITIGATION AS UNFAIR. SOCIALISM USES THE COURTS TO ADJUST INEQUITIES IN SOCIETY, THEN TO BRING JUSTICE. SOCIALISM CONVERTS LAW INTO SOCIAL MANAGEMENT, IRRESPECIVE OF THE VEHICLE—EXECUTIVE, LEGISLATIVE, JUDICIAL. Have you ever wondered about Obama's trashing of the US Constitution and the silence of Congress? In my book, that is anarchy.

The basic objection by Socialists to the Fifth Amendment is that it promotes, endorses and results in inequality of station and of means, read moneyed power. Ordinarily, there is a winner and a loser in competition. But under Socialism competition means a struggle for self-interest. Under Socialism, there is an inequitable transfer of award-money to the winner in the verdict that is to his self-interest. In the Socialist State, the disposal of money, of rewards as a result of competition means the end of competition in litigation for self-interest.

Elimination by "fixing" the outcome of the trial reduces the harmful results of selfish self-interest, read inequitable results, both to society and to the State. Therefore, to keep the impression of the continued existence of Amendment Five alive, yet to remove its thrust toward inequality by selfish court battles, the idea of due process is changed to "due exchange." Consequently the protections accorded to the accused under the old interpretation are no longer extended to the plaintiff, nay, to either party to the dispute. Both parties to a dispute, in effect, become victims. Yet both become winners. There are no losers. That is State Socialism, which we are involved in today. Appeasement of our enemies as well as reforms in our justice system will reflect this change. SOCIALISM CONSTRUES ACTIONABLE GUILT AS UNFAIR AND LITIGATION AS UNJUST BECAUSE IT SUPPORTS THE CAPITALIST CREED OF SELF-INTEREST.

The structure of double jeopardy is prohibitive, and should be removed, since a second trial can be effectively used by the State as propaganda o balance the deleterious results on the victim by the first trial. In effect, then the plaintiff becomes the person at trial replacing the defendant. Neither is an actual winner. That is to say that both are winners. The State is intolerant of moral differences in situations determined by ideology-motivated decisions . . . except any its own ideology of Socialistic fairness. Remember the Socialist's philosophy that all men are naturally good. It is the virtuous State that will reform the criminal. SOCIALISM INTENDS TO REFORM HUMAN NATURE. TO ACCOMPLISH THIS IT WILL BECOME ESSENTIALLY A POLICE STATE, TRACKING EVERYTHING YOU DO IN LIFE. THE PEOPLE ARE SOULLESS DRONES TO BE USED. Ever wonder why Washington ignores the will of the people? There are only two ultimate weapons against this oppression—the gun and the ballot box. First to go are the guns and then the effective ballots. Every push in between is talk.

The notions of a capital crime, an infamous crime is too vague to permit of keeping the idea in the Amendment and will be gradually removed. It will be redefined as a crime against the all-powerful State and is therefore a crime of conspiracy, subterversion, and insurrection of political malfeasance. To the Socialist, all crimes are against the State. The dignity and stature of the

State cannot be successfully challenged or diminished in a criminal court by this position . . .

Life, Liberty and Property are capitalist concepts. Under Socialism, personal Property is no longer of any importance in trial procedure considerations, Liberty is flexible. Life when worthy by state recognition and acceptance. All three entities come under Socialists and are therefore subject to State evaluation and control. Rationing of medical care will do much to remove respect or life consideration in the public consciousness. LIFE, LIBERTY AND THE PURSUIT OF HAPPINESS, UNDER PRESENT SOCIALISM, ARE NOW STATE GIFTS TO THE PEOPLE.

Since the Socialist State is the prime mover of lawsuits, the individual citizen having been stripped of his self-interested plea of innocence, and the power to plead as a victim before the general public, vicimizaion being scorned by the virtuous State, and the concept of the citizens right to bring a cause of action having been removed only to be replaced by the victim State, there can be no extraordinary charge of crime for murder, arson sabotage or terrorism. Therefore, the purpose of the trial court and its lawyers becomes not to convince and to defend in pursuit of a just decision, but to equitably maintain social equality of the litigants (GUILT DESTROYS THAT EQUITY) this voiding of guilt and punishment are aspects of Socialist Utopia. The reduction of crime by the oppression of "unfair" charges and by the mitigation of punishment with jobs, community service, rehabilitation means that these Socialist perks bring justice to a society.. Essentially, therefore, there can be no capital or infamous crimes. The State has changed the contributions of guilt and innocence to the status of litigant equality thus perfecting society to conform to the virtue of the Socialist State. UNDER SOCIALISM, PUNISHMENT IS MITIGATED BY VIRTUOUS ACTS OF A UTOPIAN STATE. Ever wonder why leftists and liberals want to decriminalize illegal aliens . . . as a gesture of electioneering virtue?

A Grand Jury is a capitalist invention to specialize the inequities inherent in a major criminal trial. Thus the indictment becomes an interdiction of State power into court decisions, yet an instrument that fosters inequality. The sinful nature of a murder can be rearmed and therefore his crime removed by Statist fiat.

The armed services have their own codes for adulating crimes within their ranks. These cases under a Socialist State are subject to review and revocation in the interests not of humanity but in the Statist interests of personal, moral, physical and innocence equality. A second accusation of murder is "neutralized" in the interest of State authority, the removal of any competitive inequities—as convictive evidence and prejudicial testimony—propitiated by the first trial. The State bears the costs of both trials. War by its nature is competitive and thus can be characterized as non-war, a delusion shared by all Socialists and instrumental in ambitious demonstrations against war and against American soldiers—since both sides stand in a relationship of ambitious cooperation, unfriendly juxtaposition of conflicting interests having been reduced or removed by conciliatory conversation between political enemies. SOCIALIST OBAMA ESTABLISHES A MUTUALITY OF INNOCENCE-OF-INTENT BY CONVERSING WITH DICTATORS OF THE WORLD.

The most acceptable phrase in the Fifth Amendment is that the accused shall not be a: "witness against himself." This bifurcation of testimonial fact—his corpus delecti and his testimony—and the truth of the accusation gratify the Socialist demand for equity in the Courts by the removal of the concept of trial competition, rivalry, and legal challenges of refutation by contending lawyers. This is a reflection of the major stance of the State—to promote appeasement based on the natural goodness of men. SOCIALISM'S PHILOSOPHJY OF MAN'S NATURAL GOODNESS IS THAT IT HELPS TO REDUCE PUNISHMENT THEREFORE TO REDUCE CRIME.

The last idea that a person cannot be deprived of life, liberty or property without due compensation is, in the minds of Socialists, simply foolishness. The public use is always in place and to be broadly defined in a Socialist State,; therefore this specific protection is irrelevant to honest justice. "Public use" is not a question that devolves upon the court, thus knocking out, expunging the entire Amendment purpose. Public use means use to the socialist State in contradistinction to the people, not just pragmatic use as roads and bridges but economic use as revenue, and compensatory use such as in payoffs, bribes, and settlements for political favors. These are PUBLIC USES of whatever lives maybe taken, i.e. fined or taxed, whatever liberties conflict with the Socialist desire of equity between all citizens, and whatever property may be taken, appropriated, confiscated for the use of the State, presumed owner in theory thereof. Radical legislation from the Bench will change the basic Constitutional meaning of "public use." PUBLIC USE IS ENLARGED TO INCLUDE REVENUES, PERSONAL PROFITS OF DEVELOPERS THEREBY, ALL CHANGES THAT WILL RESULT IN CONVENIENCE TO THE PUBLIC COME .UNDER "PUBLIC USE." This is a form of redistribution of wealth, a Marxist notion.

What we have in consideration of these voided protections is an Amendment Five that is made meaningless and impotent to protect the individual, now no longer considered a citizen in a free Constitutional Republic but a servant of the Socialist State, a drone, a serf, a unit, a soviet-style worker. Remember that Socialists are the enemy of Capitalist self-interest competition as found in the free market, as demonstrated by our history of adventure risks and investment enterprise.

SIX

SOCIALISTS MODIFY PROTECTIONS UNDER AMENDMENT VI

Citizen.

AMENDMENT 6: "In all criminal prosecutions, the accused shall enjoy the right to a speedy and public trial, by an impartial jury of the State and district where the crime shall have been committed, which district shall have been previously ascertained by law, and to be informed of the nature and cause of the accusation; to be confronted with the witnesses against him; to have compulsory process for obtaining witnesses in his favor; and to have the Assistance of Counsel for his defense." These protections are God-given rights. They are not State-invented and State-delegated privileges.

THE PEOPLE MUST BECOME AWARE OF THE CONTINUATION OF PRESIDENT OBAMA'S "TRANSFORMATION" OF AMERICA. The originalist interpretation of this Amendment is simple: a citizen accused of a crime shall have certain rights, endowed upon him by their Creator, in an action at bar IMMEDIATE, PUBLIC trial, WITNESSES against and for to appear in court; and the assistance of COUNSEL. Those four. Secrecy whether by the Congress or by the Court is a curse to a working democracy and the perversion of justice for the innocent. Take note 111th Congress. The trial must be public. Delay results in loss or destruction of evidence, disappearance of witnesses and changes in the economy that affect use of the court system. Furloughed judges, closed courthouses.

Under Socialism, the pleadings are controlled by the State. Denial of guilt is equivalent to assumption of innocence, Witnesses for and witnesses against may not be so identified in order to avoid the context of competition by lawyers in the self-interest of the accused client or to the detriment of the plaintiff. The thrust and determination of the trial is to achieve fairness, not by counsel's proving the validity and applicability of facts surrounding the crime and accusation, but by the opinion and the prerogative of the presiding liberal judge. While the jurors sit as traditional hearers of the facts, to parrot the State's ambition for fairness, the judge is responsible not only for stating the law in the case, but for rendering a liberal appraisal of the evidence in the interest not of the accused but of the State. This redefining of judge-jury objectives results in a trial that more resembles a hearing than it does a traditional trial. In effect, the judge removes from the jurors the pressure of responsibility for appraisal and evaluation of the facts of the case. Yet he or she, as a State employee, in his instructions to the jurors, allows them to respond to their personal feelings and opinions as their best guides for a conscionable verdict. The heart is always the best guide in these circumstances. The natural goodness of human nature must dominate the outcome. If, for example, the jury cannot reach a heat-felt decision, the judge with his superior moral virtue must step in and make whatever adjustments are necessary to present a "fair trial" to society.

The State through the judge controls jury selection—formerly done by the contending lawyers—to avoid the onerous wrongs seen under Socialism to be the plague of capitalist intrigue and lawyer competition. These sorts of competition are not worthy of a Socialist court and should be outlawed. Also, the State, by its public employee Attorney General alone—and not the jury—fixes the nature and amount of the award.

The speed of the trial is irrelevant. The accused may be kept in limbo for a long time, a year, two years, during which time his life is on hold. However, he is admonished to think of others and not just himself. The reasoning is that every man deserves his day in court, a prospect viewed as an Entitlement which the citizen feels obliged to take advantage of—like free medical care—whatever the charge or complaint . . . a :real "people's court" at last. Every citizen can then say: Justice is "my way."
The assumption of guilt, a European idea, protects the State from the inclusion, the introduction of evidence detrimental to the State's position, which is one of virtuous neutrality.

Under Socialism, the location of the crime is no longer of any relevance, it being assumed that Statist powers are broad spread and non-negotiable with respect to location of the crime.

No use of the word "alleged" is to be permitted in any of the documents, it being the mandate of the State that all facts pertinent to the crime are fixed, final and confirmed by the State as pre-dispersive of justice.

Hearsay evidence is conditionally permitted, the Socialist argument being that the witness speaks the truth as best he knows it, the judge being the final arbiter to discriminate the kind, nature, quality and content of the testimony as a State employee. Loyalty trumps the truth. The free press learned that long ago.

The impartiality and protection of the original conditions of innocence, confrontation, and State selection of witnesses—as in recruiting for army service—witnesses now rests in the hands of the morally virtuous Statist judge. What marks this type of "hearing" trial from the originalist sort of trial is that the State is now the arbiter of the conflicting testimony, facts and assumptions, if there are any conflicts, to be resolved in the following manner:
No competition between lawyers as to cause or causes of the litigation
No assignment or assumption of guilt of the accused.
No introduction of facts that place the defendant accused in a position of contention with society, as well as with the plaintiff.

All relevant evidence is to be neutralized so as to make it plausibly applicable both to the perpetrator of the crime and the victim of the crime. Under Socialism, every man is the moral equal of his neighbor; no man can complain of or contend against a government that is morally virtuous. By this reasoning, the onerous burden to society of crime is removed and in the interest of reform, the citizen is counseled as if he had committed no crime or a very small crime. This Socialist purification of society is a relativist concept found in its construction of the ideal police state. Electronic surveillance makes this a feasible objective nowadays. This moral purification and salutary improvement of mankind generally under Socialism saves the State enormous amounts of incarceration costs and projects its glowing ambition to reform as many would-be criminals as is possible in the interest of community virtue.

The State makes the judge the sole decider of any monetary awards. Monies exacted as penalties or fines shall be evenly distributed between the accused and the plaintiff, to modify the nature, the cause and the pain of the outcome if the accused is found to be\without cause, as is appropriate under Socialism.

Finally, the protections, formerly so-called under Republicanism, of this Amendment shall not apply when the accused contends for his innocence, this status having been determined by interrogation before trial, by testimony on the stand, and through observation by neutral witnesses for the State. Self-interest, a Capitalist creed, is thereby eliminated in the interests of justice and comity in the community.

SEVEN

SOCIALIST LITIGATION UNDER SEVENTH AMENDMENT

Citizen.

Socialism abridges the law of contracts by removing parity, a thing of value in exchange for another thing of value. This type of contract is deleterious to the Socialist dicta of equivalence in all contracts and negotiations at common law. Contract law in effect enriches the powerful, enabling them to live in penthouses, while the losers, the poor middle-class, return to their squalorous crumbling hovels. (Alinsky-Obama) Contracts are therefore destructive of a fair society and keep the losers perpetually in penury and squalor.

This ideological construct animated Obama to crash GM and by extra-Constitutional (outside) authority to mandate the 787 billion dollar bailout, even as the Socialist ideology continues to energize his further seizures and bankrupting of Americas civil and financial institutions. Alinsky warned him not be specific in takeovers but to include including schools and churches and charities.

Therefore, contesting litigation is unacceptable in a State Court; with or without a jury In other words, discursive negotiations must be the rule in a Socialist environment . . . Especially when the State is dealing with the enemy, Capitalists Republican Conservatives. The citizen cannot sue to collect a living-wage judgment, since such awards are contrary to the standing State morality of fairness, as written in the media. Any jury award that transgresses that dictum is and should be abolished by the Department of Justice. It is the Socialist Judge who must decide upon the award and its equitable distribution. The old-time Capitalist method of court awards makes the individual winner-recipient superior to the State in rights and powers of control.

Socialism makes award money instead of one-sided justice the leveler of the playing field. Ever watchful to protect its rights, the State cannot either tolerate or permit the immoral and often unethical transgression of controversial litigation. Justice is the essence of a heartfelt ruling by the Magistrate. And so it should be in any litigious disagreement. The disagreement is human; the solution is a virtuous and moral Petition. Under Capitalism the prejudice found in one-sided awards to the winner of a controversy can be disastrous to a fair trial. Therefore, award money defined and distributed equitably to both sides by the presiding Judge, both winners in the eyes of the State, is an absolute requirement for advancing the cause of justice in America.

AMENDMENT 7: "In Suits at common law, where value in controversy shall exceed twenty dollars, the right to trial by jury shall be preserved, and no fact tried by a jury shall be otherwise reexamined in any Court of the United States, than according to the rules of the common law." The reexamination occurs in a Court of Appeals. The fact is not stricken from the record by a trial judge or upon petition by an attorney on the case.

This protection of a citizen's innocence by a jury trial applies only to one set of circumstances, money in controversy. What about property ownership, slander or libel, inheritance moneys, business ownership and CEO authority. There are many other contests to be determined by the judge. The Socialists must regulate these entities as threats to their solution of problems encountered by the poor and disentranced. These issues are the spinoffs of a materialistic society, of the Haves in conflict with the Have-Nots, and the Would-Be-Have-Nots with the Would-Haves-Mores. It is the responsibility and the power accorded to him or her that the judge control any contests over 20 dollars. By reassessing the value of the winning side the State—selected Judge is forced by the Doctrine of Distribution to share the award with the losing side.

The jury trial gives the Judge an opportunity to erase certain status quo injustices by his or her ruling, like a purser, and to substitute orthodoxy of fairness that shall benefit both sides to the litigation. The State will always back up, support and reinforce the Justice in such cases, for it has a vested interest in the welfare of the poor. The ruling by the Justice must always be a heartfelt ruling that complies with conscience and extends the hand of fellowship to the poor and suffering of society. Jury Trial must be, under Socialist doctrine, an instrument of revelation and wealth equalizing force in such cases.

Under Socialism, the status quo is a curse to our society. President Obama has said as much as a community organizer. His mentor Saul Alinsky of Chicago thuggery has said the same. How in American society the status quo ever arrived at its present state of vital opulence and productive richness is never revealed by the middle-class disgruntled poor who are suspicious of democracy, as championed by dictators of the world. Obama applauds them so as to discourse about their political success in distributing national wealth, sometimes called dictatorship over the people and absolute control over the economy . . .

DISCLAIMER: This reinterpretation of Amendment VII is intended to show that Socialists construe the State and not God to be the source of our "inalienable" Bill of Rights. They have changed the source to suit their preferences and their grasp of power as a means, they believe, to benefit the people. They eschew Capitalism as a greedy surrogate for God and condemn Capitalists as selfish mongers of personal acquisition, to the detriment of the people generally. President Obama excludes himself from this group, being a Marxist leftist of the Alinsky persuasion (change means revolution) who believes, by words and not his actions, that his brilliance outshines the wisdom of Washing, Jefferson, Madison, Adams and all the signers of the Declaration of Independence and of the US Constitution, combined! They were wrong; he is right.

The Socialists, having reconstructed the nature of Rights, have done so these past eighteen months in order to reassure the people that a Right is identical to an Entitlement, the latter word being more readily understood by a people deprived of elementary school education and therefore more malleable by the greedy Capitalist penthouse structuring of America's Capitalist elitists. The present Administration continues to purvey this colossal dark lie of Socialist superiority while they increase their control and enlarge the government at will. Obama is a do-nothing propagandist, failure as a President, and a scourge on this country's past and its future.

The Socialist tack and these views are the vendetta of President Barrack Hussein Obama—who detests America. They are also the views of his virtuous cabinet of leftist parasite surrogates and, parenthetically, they are the views and the convictions of the mainstream Socialist media who appear to be the purveyors of truth but are, in fact, the denigrators and the obliterators and the concealors of the truth in the name of news . . . particularly the last.

These corrupt parasites, including Czars and other Cabinet heads of known and of invented offices, are bent upon the destruction of Constitutional Republican America, replacing it with an artificial, ideologically contrived edifice of government that will fail—as it has failed everywhere else in the world—and that will bring about this nation's total collapse economically, politically and socially. The Church, having been infiltrated by leftists, will not stand, as in Fascist Germany of the 1930's. America and her people will become the property of creditor communist Red China and the borrowed mouthpiece of Continental Europe. We will become the pawn of the UN. If we do not expunge this administration and its evil ideology at the ballot box, we will once again have to fight for freedom with guns in the streets. That is the only power tyrants understand. Obama and his leftist surrogate supporters are tyrants, concealed behind democratic names.

The American people will neither submit nor be silenced. It will be a fiercer fight than it was against the British—also a revolutionary civil war—because we will remember our history and our greatness and our struggles and our faith, and we will not be placated by political rhetoric or made dumb by regulations, or intimidated by threats to submit and to become servants to government masters. The touch fire will be widespread adult hunger in the streets that gathers impetus by concerted robberies of food from markets in America's major cities. The police will make a sign of opposition but they will step aside when they see the cause. Obama will ride like royalty through the streets of Washington, DC. in a golf cart shouting "let them eat pizzas!"

Will we have men of character like our Founders—which has to include women like Martha and Dolly—to reconstruct a similar free nation as they did in Philadelphia in 1789? As a blood descendant of certain of those great men who fought for liberty, I am skeptical. Likewise, I do no fear to fight, first with a ballot and, if it becomes necessary, with a gun for the same God-given Rights.

EIGHT

SOCIALISTS ABHOR EXCESSIVE FINES AND STUPENDOUS BAIL

Citizen:

The Leftists and radical liberals are offended by heavy fines for three reasons. (1) an excessive bail or fine discourages free enterprise by the mechanism of fear that such court-imposed mathematics impose on law breakers. (2) the power to control shifts from the court to the bail bondsman, from State employee to private entrepreneur; and (3) reduction in worker efficiency occurs when bail becomes too much to repay.

This is the one Amendment that the Socialists approve of because it appears to conform to their doctrine that wealth should not become concentrated in the hands of too few persons, whether lesser authority figures or entrepreneurs. The State alone shall be the source, protector and distributor of wealth among the people. That is the solid basic doctrine that sustains Socialism as a gratuitous way of life. The Capitalist greed to amass wealth into the hands of a few penthouse dwellers corrupts the entire society by keeping the poor disenfranchised and forcing them to live in their crumbling shacks. That is both an unfair and perverse accounting for a nation's wealth.

AMENDMENT 8: Excessive bail shall not be required, nor excessive fines imposed, nor cruel and unusual punishment inflicted." The thrust of this amendment is to preserve the sense and reality of freedom for men who fought for their personal liberty and the rational deliverance of a free state elected by the people. They were tired of Crown fines for little cause, of excessive taxes the last of which, the Stamp Tax (repealed), and ignited the Revolution. They were exhausted by the Parliament's implacable and endless tariffs and duties imposed on products made by their own hands. When it came to the imposition of fines, this Amendment VIII was their answer.

The Amendment, therefore, protects the citizen economically, which pleases the Socialists. It also protects him physically from dangerous and injurious sorts of punishment, a specialty of the Crown government. Drawing and quartering, for example, was commonly imposed as a bloody penalty for the mere theft of a loaf of bread. One can therefore, understand the Colonial retributive punishment of tarring and feathering and riding the tax collectors out of town on a rail and setting fire to his house. The two changes the Socialists would make to the Amendments (1) that the Judge be a State employee and (2) that the bail bondsman also be employed by the State. In either case, the State maintains control on the flow of money regardless of its source, its distribution being left to the Government's discretionary power.

President Obama's agenda is his vendetta to cut down penthouse figures to size like GM's CEO, and to redistribute the wealth gotten thereby to the millions who live in crumbling hovels, according to Saul Alinsky. This wins him Messianic acclaim world-wide and demonstrates the veracity of his conviction that America's penthouse figures—he always excludes himself—have impoverished the rest of the world. The oil damage to Gulf shores and marshland is the just retribution by a compassionate God. Why should he hurry? His concern is sheer propaganda. Offers by the Dutch and twelve other nations to help was of little value to the tyrant of the circumstances, President Obama. He could not have endured the reduction or overshadow of his narcissistic pride to admit the help of an experienced nation.

The Eighth Amendment acknowledges the gift and the positive aspects of freedom for the newly liberated Britton, ACCUSED OF MISDEMEANOR OR A CRIME, and now a citizen of a new country to be called The United States. Cruel and unusual punishments are Feudal in nature, depending as they do on the wicked nature of natural man and in collusion with the power of the State.

Excessive bail and fines belonged to a corrupt Parliament and King, who saw the colonies as a burden only to be reimbursed by heavy duties on products from their own hands. The Colonists were tired and fed up with heavy fines imposed on the people for minor offenses, like failing to salute the British flag when carried by a cadre of British troops through a colonial town. Or physical opposition to quartering British soldiers . . . .

Under Socialism, the priests and followers of this Socialist ideology would, in fact, strike out this Amendment VIII entirely from the list of Ten; simply because it (a) transgresses sanity by the acknowledgement of any bail whatsoever. Yet the Socialist doctrine of State arbiter dictum being applied would release all prisoners into society and punish none with monetary fines, as opposed to the punishment of hard labor. (b) and would simply ignore the matter of bail and fines altogether, because, under Socialism, such imposed demands for money conflict with the Socialist doctrine of wealth distribution and equality of income earnings, therefore subject to State requirement and demand for compliant distribution of income. There can be neither at the same time, demand and distribution. Therefore, the former must go. Unequal incomes by the middle class reflect the defiant self-interest that punishes the poor by denials of food, which the State must compensate for Strict regulation will eliminate these inequalities of income and living conditions. In Soviet Russia, liquidation of independent farmers was the resolution to defiance.

This riddance, however, leaves crime without a punishment—being virtuous and the source of virtue, the State can commit no crimes—and makes the very notion of guilt offensive to the State. In the New Utopia envisioned under Socialism, guilt and punishment are an anathema to the new State. The intrusion of money simply reinforces the letter of the doctrine of punishment that fits the crime. Where a heinous crime has been committed, the State shall dispose of the culprit in silence and or by exile, the ignominious riddance from the country.

Therefore, the eradication of money from all consideration and the restoration thereby of the innocence of the alleged offender is the positive offshoot of the elimination of this amendment altogether from the Bill of Rights. The Rights of slack fines and little punishment that can be called cruel is simply a statement of freedom, given to the citizen not by

God but by the State. For it was the State that engaged the Crown in the Revolution, not God, was it not? Therefore the fruits of that struggle must be held, tendered and supplied by the State. There is no other way to achieve equality of wealth and political power. The State shall be the surpra-orbiter of the entire process of fines and punishment to protect the life and happiness of the individual.

Monies from fines shall be distributed among the poor. Therefore, there can be no limit on the maximum level of the fine or the bail. There can be no concentration, acquisition, possession or amassing of trial monies gotten from bail and fines that remains in the hand of one citizen, lest such a reprehensible procedure violate the Socialist mandate of ULTIMATE EQUALITY OF BANK ACCOUNTS. The personal bank account is essentially an instrument of investment Capitalism. It is used for investment in order to increase the size of the account which acquisition is by motive and selfish greed becomes an instrument of unfair! and inequitable wealth.

The Socialists leaders will use electronic access to the bank accounts of citizens in the Socialist State. This State freedom of access will largely eliminate that Capitalist abhorrent disgrace to a free society. The State will manage, control and regulate the power of investment. This action will absolve the people from future transgressions—secular salvation of future forgiveness—that will, in turn, make Amendment VIII irrelevant to the New World utopian society.

NINE

SOCIALISTS VIOLATE AMENDMENT NINE BY "DISPARAGE" RIGHTS RETAINED BY THE PEOPLE.

AMENDMENT 9: "The enumeration in the Constitution of certain rights shall not be construed to deny or disparage others retained by the people." This Amendment opens the way to fraud and special interests yet, at the same time, protects the people from oppressive government in the face of their individual liberties.

Among those "retained by the people." the State construes the present to be wrong for example in the matter of condoms, the State denies the parents this power to instruct their child, and the State disparages that right as a parental prerogative. The State, therefore, replaces God by admonition in the training and upbringing of the child. What if "good citizenship" is today a Statist possessory interest, when civics is no longer taught and America and American History is corrupted by pop culture?

The intent of this Amendment of the Bill of Rights is to extend the endowed rights by God to other rights not mentioned in the First Ten, but that appear as a continuations of the Right to amend the Constitution, the Right to be free, the Right to vote, endowed upon all citizens. Ancillary rights issue from the initial Bill of enumerated rights has been construed by the Supreme Court as Civil Rights. These repose by implication and are therefore ancillary to the first ten and that, likewise, cannot be infringed upon or abridged.

Socialists find these ancillary rights fertile means to extend their power over the people, construing these rights, as to privacy, equality of treatment in the courts, as having come from the State rather than from God. Important among these ancillary rights is the primary right of the parents to govern their progeny, superseding the right of the State in matters of education, for example. In earlier days children were withdrawn school to help on the family farm. The State was then powerless. Now the State plays the role of an omnipotent parent.

In millions of families, the State has usurped the power of parental control over their children in the matter of sex education. This is illegal, immoral and divisive of parental control over their children. The socialists find this control, this shift of control from parents to State, exemplary, fruitful and necessary to the enlargement of its power. Parents and the church stand in the way of Government assuming powers to control worship . . . if ;not faith, and the sex education of the next generation. Children under this shift in power become mindless units, whose morality\y will be the issue of the State to decide instead of the parents. The State, the Socialist State, considers itself virtuous and therefore qualified to administer advice . . . irrespective of parental decisions or opinion. The State is disdainful of parental control. When the state assumes control of the child, that child then is subjected to State indoctrination, which has happened in sex education, irrespective of religious intercession by the parents. The Constitution does not give the Sate the right under Amendment IX to disparage the right of the parent to educate the child in matters of moral conduct. Therefore, the socialists violate this Amendment IX in their usurpation of parental power. They do not Constitutionally possess this power of interposition between parent and child. The Socialist State will use every device to take over the parental role—neglect, child abuse, drugs, impoverishment, child endangerment, sex education, omission of parental advice and decisions, abandonment . . . .

The state, therefore, places itself between the parents and the child and in doing so becomes the trainer, the surrogate parent, of the child outside the classroom, invading the home to usurp the authority of parents.
Here is a brief list of Statist power grabbing controls over the people's Constitutional God-given rights:—

How many children parents shall have:—suggested by—Red China that fines parents for more than one child/ CONSTITUTIONAL; AUTHORITY? Parents and the Catholic Church have the right to choose the numbers of children in a family. The State is morally out of the picture. Not so nowadays, in Red China and, coming soon, in the United States. This right is implied in Amendment IX. The State's interest is to train the child either to be a member of an army or a willing servant of the State as a brainwashed bureaucrat. There is no thought given to the child's or the children's individuality.

Religious instruction in the home is abrogated by sex instruction in the schools, What is the CONSTITUTIONAL AUTHORITY for this suppression of parental right to teach their children about sex and to be the only source of such instruction? Are we to introduce a JOY IN LIFE venue as in Fascist Germany in order to rear a generation of bastards useful to the State?

Fatty foods in home prohibited. What is the CONSTITUT AUTHORITY? Diet is another right that is protected by the inviolable authority of parents in the home-rearing of their children. Such a statute will attempt to take over that right in order to increase its Statist power. Home-schooling has come about as a reaction to Statist control of education in public schools. The equalization of conduct, competency and treatment of individual's natural abilities in collectivistic classrooms has led to mediocrity in performance.

Parental discipline of the child is referred to the child abuse agency. What is the CONSTITUTIONAL AUTHORITY for such usurpation of parental control of their progeny?

Limits on homework is, again, made a matter of child abuse and the usurpation of parental authority within the home—a IX retained right

Privacy—abortion is a right retained by the people under Amendment IX. The State, or money and power, has made the woman's privacy a regulatory and revenue matter. Neither life per se nor the women are of any intrinsic value before and after the State's seizure of this protected right.

The Right to work if able and can find a job at present is a motif of politics. What is the State's CONSTITUTIONALAUTHORTY? .Society can function only by the labor of its citizens. The State is not empowered to flaunt that truism, yet it has no Constitutional authority on its own initiative to command business and shops to shut down as if to protect it and the people from the spread of a disease—perhaps the only justification for doing so. . . . not for profit-sharing. Obama acted unconstitutionally when he crashed GM, took over certain investment houses as AIG, ordered student loans to be single-sourced . . . all Socialist takeover moves that were decidedly unconstitutional. Cite the CONSITUTIOAL AUTHORITY. Such outlawry is characteristic of this administration. Again, the right to work is protected by Amendment IX

Right of freedom of association, a tyrant's second target for destruction because it threatens his power as a potentially subversive. Cite CONSTITUT. AUTHORITY? Civil rights activists are in for a surprise. However, under Amendment I, the right of the people "peaceably to assemble" protects the right of association, Two are an assembly.

Child's authority over parents—a growing anxiety CONSTITUTIONAL AUTHORITY? Parents not the State retain the exclusive right, under amendment IX—to rear their children. That is a right retained by the people. "Child abuse" is a Statist standard, not a biblical standard. The right to discipline the child is a right "retained by the people. The Constitution Identifies the child as an individual, not as a Statist object for exploitation. That is a Statist concept designed to rear armies for the State.

Self-defense under all circumstances abridged against CONSTITUTIONAL AUTHORITY?. The individual's right to self-protection under Amendment It means the purposeful possession of arms. A citizen's right to protect himself and his home is not abrogated by the authority of the State to delegate that protection to the police. The precedent is being set in the Arizona immigration law. If that singular self-protective right is not in place and honored by the Socialist State, the city can bring suit against a defending homeowner for transgressing police protective power!

Shop-closing time, by what CONSTITUTIOAL AUTHORLITY? Entrepreneur's rejection of the law is protected by Amendment IX. The Right of the people engaged in making a profit is a right to create, to prosper, an inalienable right referred to as a means to happiness. See the Declaration of Independence.

Mandatory vacation . . . under CONSTITITUION AUTHORITY? The citizen retains the right to fix his sown times for work and recreation, under Amendment IX. Try to enforce this as a societal law and you will prove yourself evil, felonious and a threat to the continued existence of a free society. In Europe, the law prevails because it equalizes income of shopkeepers! Stupid fools!.

In all of the above controls there exists no authority under our Constitution for the above State actions. but every authority and protection for retention of the Rights is assured to Parents, Entrepreneurs and Individuals under our Constitution. All of the above intrusions of the State represent government seizures are denials and disparagements of rights retained by the people under Amendments I, II & IX. Therefore, the above seizures and controls are unconstitutional and tyrannical. You, as a citizen do not have to obey the government when that government transgresses the US Constitution. You do not willfully by conscience have to obey lawlessness and thus become complicit in the unlawful act. Held up in a stage coach by a highwayman, you obey but at the point of a gun. Held up by an un-Constitutional Supreme Court ruling, read piece of heart-felt "living: legislation, disobey, resist, fight. even at your peril. The Court is not above the law and it is not a law in action for the common people if you do not comprehend its meaning and its consequences. Next time that that Obama fraud; attempts to take over an industry, trashing contracts, stand up to his destructive abuse of power. All but two of the above rights are ancillary rights endowed upon the people by their Creator. If you are not a believer, you enjoy them by God's general grace. They are not the creations and issue of the Socialist State.

PRESIDENT BARACK OBAMA IS AN ANTI-CONSTITUTIONAL OUTLAW. No person is safe in his person, job or home while he is in office. Obama thinks, in his revelry against the law, that he is invincible. That arrogant assumption is dangerous to America and to Americans . . . of whom he is not one, being a cotower to our enemies and an insulter to our friends. He does not want to be identified as an American. He wants to distance himself from the people. He has proved now that he detests this great nation. How? By breaking its fundamental structural and preservation Law of the Constitution, in violation of his oath, of office, yet another lie. He is an AMERICAN-ITE and just as equally a Mammon-ite Socialist. He thinks to convert America into a virtuous nation in emulation of himself. You lie contemptuously against our history, sir. The virtuous State, it follows, endows the citizen with a sense of his innate goodness and therefore removes two things: (1) a sense of his obligations to society; and (2) the reality of sin and therefore of his guilt before the law of the State, as compared to his guile before a Holy God.

TEN

SOCIALISTS SEIZE TENTH AMENDMENT, PEOPLE IRRELEVANT TO THEIR POWER

Citizen.

AMENDMENT 10:—"The powers not delegated to the United States by the Constriction, nor prohibited by it to the States, are reserved to the States respectively or to the people."

The curious statement in this Amendment X is the RESERVED . . . THE PEOPLE—other rights not enumerated or inferred in the first nine amendments. That clause indicates that the people hold in their care a power to enact self-protective rights, acknowledgement of and acceptance of the fact that the Bill of Rights was and is designed to protect the people from the Federal Government/

One of those RESERVED right is the right of a state to protect itself from physical assault, from invasion, as is occurring in Arizona, the cause of which gave rise the State law 1070. All entities that consider and pursue a retribution of The state, under the circumstances of its border assaults, cannot stand idly by and must, and has the right to, protect its citizens with this law, under this Amendment. The right and the power of self defense, is by this amendment extended both to a political entity, the state, and to the person, a citizen.

If the radicals in our present government can isolate enumerated rights and show because why they endanger our free society, they need no verbal reference to those "reserved" rights, because the radicals in the administration and in Congress will have removed from us the protection of those enumerated rights. Thus liberated thoroughly from the Bill of Rights, the Supreme Court will only appear to administer due process. Obama once remarked in a comment that that Process is unnecessary. That transformation of our judicial system is what Obama and his radicalized Supreme Court intends, with the help of the know-nothings in the media and with the cooperation, surprisingly, of the protestant churches in America. Elimination of religious expression from the public forum has bee under way since the 1960's. Classification of churches as corporations will begin the assault on religious freedom by regulatory controls. Regulations have already stifled home churches in American communities—but not in China!

Due process if ever it should be abridged by a radical court, would lead the way to the extinction of enumerated protections, and silence the honor and voice of the people that will no longer be operative to freedom because it will have become, to the state, the voice of dead works. The conscience mentioned by Paul in 2nd Corinthians and in ancient Hebrews of the New Testament (cf: Strong's Concordance) would fail to be of any value in courts of law, as discerning argument to defend an enumerated Right. The virtuous State bestows goodness, if not innocence on its citizens. . God acknowledges Man's innate sinfulness. The effectiveness and efficiency of the Nazi SS was achieved by men without a conscience, moral discernment having been destroyed by State brainwashing—Hitler's intention e.g., to raise a generation without a conscience..

A moral conscience and a political right are inseparably linked. For that reason, nowadays, the state is beginning to assume the mantle of virtue, thieving this token of righteousness from the extant protestant and Catholic churches (by control of abortions, proclamations of liberty from the pulpit) and the Synagogues of America. Once the State becomes morally and ethically virtuous and is so recognized by the people, there will be no ober dictum, no higher authority, to challenge and to assail the supremacy of the State, for it will have seized that preeminence of power and majesty from God Almighty. Mark me. I know how men's minds work. Therefore, the "conscience of the state|" will do away with such dead works as religious freedom, freedom of speech, freedom of assembly (association) and the other enumerated rights in the Bill of Rights. Once the enumerated rights are expunged, the retained rights come next, including the right to own property. The Kelo case has set the precedent. Congressional liberals who inform us that the Founders could not "possibly" have foreseen today's present circumstances will find cause to interpret such words as ""prohibiting the free exercise", "abridging the freedom," "unreasonable searches and seizures"—causing their basic English meanings to be reinterpreted so as to conform to "positive liberties" of the Federal Government, what the Government can do (not for) to the people—introduced as rights of the Federal Government. Dictator pro tem Barack Obama is for this fundamental change in the Constitution that will enhance and consummate his projected powers.

Due process to defend the citizen from what . . . ? The very concept of due process then becomes meaningless. With its loss will come the extinction of privileges and immunities that protect the citizen from the Federal Government. All these protections are linked together, so that when one of those rights enumerated in amendment II is extinguished by a liberal court ruling, the total protection of the Bill of Rights is on the way to extinction, Right by Right, privileged by privilege, immunity by immunity. Thank God the Court in its recent decision retained the right of gun owners to keep their guns! This, of course, was a defeat for the Obama gang of pirates. Only a people desperately ignorant of or intimidated by big government or destroyed by their own self-will to illiteracy . . . illiteracy affects 20% of today's adult population . . . are vulnerable to the loss of their Creator—endowed rights. Inroads into freedom of religion will be preceded by inroads into freedom of speech in the name of feelings, self-esteem, equality of judgment, relativism of opinion and a politically-correct anarchy of social control by speech control. You might have to assemble in your bathrooms to discuss politics, as happened in Hitler's Europe. Perhaps even today.

Therefore, remove rights one by one, those enumerated in the Bill of Rights. and then, logically—explained to the dumber-down people as "dangerous" to their illiterate society—"negative liberties", those enumerated rights, once they are gone, will make of those "retained" an illusion that is easily expunged by liberal feel-good court rulings, based on German, French, Venezuela, Dutch laws. This destruction of our Constitutional protections for the citizen, those "negative liberties," will be deemed—that word again—to have been held by a people who cling to their religion and their guns. Such debasing ingratitude will appear despicable and unspeakably ugly to those who love liberty.

Obama and the socialists will point out that they gave due process a chance and it failed to protect, thus many Americans will be disenfranchised because of their political opinions. The state will now assume the role of protector that replaces the people's once—enumerated Rights. The "democratic" sloganeering will go something like this: Vote for your protectorate in Washington. They are dependable, they are responsible leaders.

"Candidate" will become a banned word. The word does not belong in a living constitution; it leads to inequalities and to racist discrimination. "Candidate" is award that connotes a bad feeling of opposition. Purge the word! See voting poll Oversight Manager to fill out your ballot. (As in some unions, no secret ballots.) The Czar will help you to select the right leader. Have confidence. You did not want to learn English or to finish your education. In your face, illiterates! The entire voting process will be regulated and controlled for efficiency and by permission of the office of voters held by that Czar appointed by Barack Obama or his lapdog successor. You won't have a clue as to what you have lost. The word "pioneer" means discoveries in women's rights and limitations on personal income. Except for the remnants of a brilliant, productive and free society once called "America", you might as well live in Europe. There everything is already set up for you . . . Obama, Pelosi, Reid, Rahm, Axelrod et al. One problem: you won't have the luxury of the remnants over there. There will be no hospitals in Europe, Michelle, to give you half a million dollars for your name and no fantasy flights to New York to see a play. Of course, there is always the coeur d' elegance of Paris for your fashions. Unlike the French, we did not rise and flourish out of Medieval serfdom. However, we did not have a bloody eight years of Revolution without constructing a replacement of the Aristocracy (King George and Parliament) by a fundamental law known as the US Constitution.